How to Make People Laugh

Quick Strategies to Improve Humor, Develop Charisma, and Build Confidence

By: Barton Press

Copyright © 2021 by Barton Press

ALL RIGHTS RESERVED

No part of this book may be reproduced, stored in a retrieval system, or transmitted in any form or by any means, electronic, mechanical, photocopying, recording, scanning, or otherwise, without the prior written permission of the publisher.

Limit of Liability/Disclaimer of Warranty: the publisher and the author make no representations or warranties with respect to the accuracy or completeness of the contents of this work and specifically disclaim all warranties, including without limitation warranties of fitness for a particular purpose. No warranty may be created or extended by sales or promotional materials. The advice and strategies contained herein may not be suitable for every situation. This work is sold with the understanding that the publisher is not engaged in rendering medical, legal or other professional advice or services. If professional assistance is required, the services of a competent professional person should be sought. Neither the publisher nor the author shall be liable for damages arising herefrom. The fact that an individual, organization or website is referred to in this work as a citation and/or potential source of further information does not mean that the author or the publisher endorses the information the individuals, organization or website may provide or recommendations they/it may make. Further, readers should be aware that websites listed on this work may have changed or disappeared between when this work was written and when it is read.

Table of Contents

Part I: Charm Their Socks Off 1

    Chapter 1: The Allure of Charm 3

    Chapter 2: The Pull of a Social Magnet 10

    Chapter 3: Always Be Interesting 17

    Chapter 4: Dazzle and Dash 30

Part II: Confidence Is Built From Within 35

    Chapter 5: Sure I'm Sure? How to Be Positively Self-Assured 37

    Chapter 6: Breaking Down Walls to Build Up Our Confidence 46

    Chapter 7: The Key to Quell Overthinking 55

    Chapter 8: Poised and Playful 69

Part III: Joke's on You: I'm Funny! 72

    Chapter 9: Finding Humor in Every Little Thing 74

    Chapter 10: It's All in the Delivery 84

    Chapter 11: How Humor Conveys Confidence 90

Part IV: Falling Down Is the Key to Stand-Up 95

Chapter 12: The Humble Comic 97

Chapter 13: You've Got Endless Stories 99

Chapter 14: Bruised Egos Build Confidence 104

Part V: Make People Laugh 108

Chapter 15: You Can't Fake Funny 109

Chapter 16: The Importance of Humor in Relationship Building 115

Chapter 17: Choose Your Style and Run with it 120

Conclusion 127

Resources 129

Part I: Charm Their Socks Off

"Charm is the ability to make someone think that both of you are quite wonderful."
— Henri-Frédéric Amiel, Swiss Philosopher

In this section of the book, you'll learn more about the allure of charm and why we find certain people more charming than others. The power to *charm someone's socks off* is quite useful in today's society, but it should never feel or come across as a forced act.

Charm should come naturally, and by understanding more about the qualities and characteristics of charming people, you'll find that you too can be charming!

Once you have a solid grasp of charm, you'll work to build the self-confidence necessary to improve your humor. And, finally, you'll learn how to make people laugh.

So, what are you waiting for?

Let's get started!

Chapter 1: The Allure of Charm

"There's a difference between beauty and charm. A beautiful woman is one I notice. A charming woman is one who notices me." — John Erskine, American Educator

Defined as *the power or quality of giving delight or arousing admiration,* charm is quite a powerful thing to have. People <u>love</u> charming people. To be charming is to be confident, and to be confident is, well, *everything.*

But confidence can easily be coupled with arrogance—and charming people are *not* arrogant. Nor are they conceited, pompous, or overbearing. This is why others are so drawn to the most charming people in the room; *but what exactly makes someone charming?*

To have the allure of charm is to have the following characteristics, personality traits, and habits:

1. **Smile often:** When you think of the most charming person you know, what stands out? It is probably his or her dashing smile for starters! Smiling indicates happiness and kindness, and happy, kind people are people you *want* to be around. Not only do charming people smile more often, but they smile when other people smile—not in a forced way, but in a truly genuine way. Smiles are contagious, after all. But remember: Anyone can spot a fake smile, and if you must fake it, don't bother.

2. **Give back:** When you're around a charming person, think about how you feel both during and after the interaction. Generally good, *right*? Charming people know how to make others feel good, and they give people genuine compliments which make the recipients feel special. In a conversation, charming people give more than they take from the other person. They make an effort to ask questions, engage, and keep everything flowing smoothly.

3. **Expressive:** Charming people are generally more expressive than others. From talking with their hands to smiling not only with their mouths but their eyes as well, these people exude a lovely, warm, fun energy that draws everyone in. Plus, research shows those who talk with their hands are viewed as more warm, agreeable, and energetic. So, if you want to be more charming, don't be shy about expressing yourself!

4. **Not a "Debbie Downer":** Negativity is a drag, and no one wants to be around a *Debbie Downer*. Charming people are generally positive and look on the bright side of things; if you're having a bad day, a charming person will find ways to make you feel better, not worse. They don't drown in sorrow and they certainly don't spend time dwelling on fear, anxiety, or sadness. That's not to say they never have a bad day, but they won't go out of their way to bring others down with them if they do. Again, consider who draws in a crowd in a room filled with people—is it the person who is complaining about something, or the person who is excited and happy about something?

5. **Eye Contact:** Maintaining eye contact with those you're talking to is *essential* if you want to be seen as utterly charming. If you're talking with someone who is constantly looking around or who seems very distracted, you're going to feel like they don't truly care about what you have to say. Strong and constant eye contact not only conveys care and trust, but it also makes the other person feel important and worthy.

6. **Laugh often:** This *is* a book about building confidence and making others laugh, so it makes sense that the most charming people among us are not only quick to laugh but quick to make others laugh as well. And this doesn't mean that charming people have a bunch of knock-knock jokes on reserve specifically for social events. Rather, they find the humor and joy in every-day scenarios, and they're able to draw this energy out in others. Charming people don't have to work for laughter; it comes rather naturally.

Of course, this isn't an all-encompassing list of every trait a charming person has, but it's certainly a start! To be charming shouldn't mean you need to undergo a personality change; in fact, it's more in the way you present yourself and how you draw out the good in others. Being charming is about your overall energy and how you carry yourself: being attentive, charismatic, confident, sincere, and patient with others.

"Charisma is not just saying hello. It's dropping what you're doing to say hello." — Robert Brault, Author

You'll often find that the most charming people tend to draw others in at parties or other events; you may often find a crowd of people surrounding them. But consider their actions and behaviors. Charming people are not selfish, arrogant, or rude. They may draw in a crowd, but they are quick to turn the attention on others and give people space to join in. They make others feel *good,* and <u>that</u> is the true allure of charm.

Truly charming people are often described as delightful, lovable, pleasant, and endearing as well. These are all traits of a person you'd want to spend time with, right? These are people with truly magnetic, enchanting personalities; those who can cast an invisible, unwritten spell, holding our attention in crowded rooms, empty bars, or even aisle 9 at the grocery store.

These people simply have *it*—this certain *something* that makes us feel good about ourselves just for being around them. These aren't people who drone on and on about themselves just to hear themselves talk. Rather, they have *something* that compels us to seek them out because they aren't selfish.

Many of us grew up surrounded by the allure of charm, whether we knew it or not. Think about your childhood…does *Prince Charming* ring a bell? Perhaps you watched *Charmed* as you scarfed down *Lucky Charms* at the breakfast table? Charm is all around us! And it's always presented in a sparkly, lovely fashion. To have charm is to have positive energy in your life. In fact, Hollywood presents us with lists of the *most charming* people—Johnny Depp was once named the "Most Charming Man Alive."

A bit mysterious, a bit elusive, charm is still attainable for those of us who aren't in the spotlight. But, what does it mean to really *draw* people in and be a social magnet who pulls others in? What's important and significant about charm in social settings? We'll dive deeper into exploring answers to these questions and more in the following chapters.

Chapter 2: The Pull of a Social Magnet

"By behaving naturally and sincerely, you become a giant magnet, pulling people to yourself!"
— Mehmet Murat İldan, Turkish Writer

For a moment, I want you to consider the pull of a magnet; magnets are only drawn to each other when unlike poles are held together. In this sense, *opposites attract*. That can be true of social magnetism as well. Humans are often intrigued and drawn to things that are different from them and truly unique. It's how we learn more about the world and ourselves in return. In fact, how we react to different people and situations can show us a lot about ourselves.

While we may be comforted by the same routines in our own day-to-day lives, we seek out entertainment through those who are confident enough to provide what's *different*. We are drawn to these societal charmers who have the pull and power to bring us joy and happiness. Think about what you do for fun: the shows you see, perhaps plays or movies, or even the circus. You're seeking an escape from your daily reality.

Perhaps writer Lukas Schwekendiek answered it best when he was once asked **What makes people charming?**

He responded:

"What makes someone charming is] the ability to see something or be something others can't. People that are charmingcan gain a deeper sense of the person in front of them or those that have a deeper sense of who they are. They often invest in the conversation deeply, keep in mind what matters to the person in front of them and can relate that to them in a very honest, direct and deep way without it seeming so. Basically, charming people understand. Charming people understand themselves, not needing to change who they are, or they

understand others, often more than they do themselves.

This sense of understanding allows them to seem incredibly genuine and free as opposed to those that put up barriers around themselves or those that pretend they understand others, but only do so seeing through colored glasses. When you talk with a charming person that understands themselves, for instance, it feels like a gust of fresh air. Talking to them feels very free. Clean. Easy. They do not pretend, and do not hide, and that makes it easy to go to deep levels with them.

It's just, overall, a very unburdened conversation that you have with them that you are being pulled into. This freedom that they bring to the conversations and the clarity is something most of us desire, bringing with it a tiny sense of jealousy at times. Children often have this sort of charm; although it is not as powerful as in adults, as we sort of expect children to be this free. On the other hand, when *you talk with a charming person that understands you on a deeper level it feels more like a comfortable knife. They pierce right through your barriers, but do it in such a way that it isn't a hard, fleshy or messy cut. It does not feel forced.*

More like a knife cutting through the surface of the water, they peer right into who you really are, seemingly with your permission but at least without your resistance. While this can be unsettling to some, to most people it often feels relieving as they start to feel truly understood. We get this sense through their ability to lead our clouded, acute, problem-driven thoughts to a bigger, overarching picture that puts it all together. You have to understand that people that are charming are so because they, in a sense, are clear. There is no sense of urgency or confusion when you talk to them. They understand, and their understanding is pure. And while they may not be this way in every aspect of their lives, as long as they are this way when they talk to you, they are charming."

Social magnets don't have to do much to pull people into their orb. Again, think about really strong magnets: there's no need to force them together to get them to really stick. In fact, you can hold them quite far apart and the energy alone will draw them together. And, once stuck, it can be quite difficult to pull them apart.

Charming people don't have to work hard or put up a front to draw others into their magnetic field. We, as observers, willingly enter their orbits of charm! And often we don't willingly want to leave the side of these charmers, much like the strong hold of a magnet. We're stuck until forced apart!

Let's consider the alternative. We've discussed how opposites attract and how people are drawn to the magnetism of charming people *because* they are different. We know that the same sides of two magnets will *not* cling to each other. While we often get along with people similar to ourselves, it can be off-putting if someone is so clearly copying or mirroring whatever other people say. As Schwekendiek said, charming folks are like a "gust of fresh air." They bring something <u>new</u> to the table. These people make us go, *oh, I never thought of it that way*, or *I had no idea anyone could do that!*

Charm is *not* the art of copying someone else; in fact, it's the opposite of that. Charm is knowing, owning, and celebrating your unique differences. And this also translates to confidence; a real, genuine confidence. No one wants to be around someone else who mindlessly agrees with every single thing someone else says. That's not charming—that's just *annoying*. If you're just a parrot, repeating those around you just to try and absorb some charm of your own, it comes off as if you're trying too hard. And that ultimately translates into *inauthenticity*. And if you're always agreeing with everyone else, then you're not a very interesting person, are you?

Charming people are extremely interesting and, of course, that's what makes them so alluring. We don't want to spend our time with boring people who have nothing original to contribute to an event or conversation. Next time you're around a charming social magnet, take special note of the way they carry themselves and the stories they're telling. Observe how others react to them. *What is it about this person*?

As Schwekendiek wrote, you may find a "childlike clarity" and freedom about these people; there's no need to pretend or hide anything. They just are who they are, and they say what they say. And others appreciate that *so* much because, in a sense, it's rarer to find these qualities in adulthood.

Talking with and listening to a rather charming person, you'll find, is clean and easy. Again, like the pull of a magnet. No mess, no fuss; just a clean pull toward this entrancing person.

In the next chapter, we'll discuss how to always be interesting–even when you think you're not! This will also help you to build confidence. Everyone has a story to tell, and we all have something to say. As long as you remember this, you'll be ready for any social situation you find yourself in; fear less, charm more!

Chapter 3: Always Be Interesting

"Have you ever noticed how the most intriguing individual in the room seems content to listen sooner than speak?" — Richelle E. Goodrich, Author

The idea of having to *always* be interesting can be overwhelming...especially if you believe you're not an inherently interesting person. But every single person has *something*—usually bunches and bunches of things, actually—that makes them unique and fascinating to others. There may be aspects of your life story that you don't find particularly engrossing, but others would find captivating.

You may never know though if you just *assume* you're not interesting and keep everything inside. And, thanks to the late comedy writer Jerry Belson, we all know to "never ASSUME, because when you assume, you make an ASS of U and ME."

Consider this: Someone comes up to you right now and says, *can you tell me something interesting about yourself?* What comes to mind? Quick, don't overthink it! Are you panicking? Do you have anything interesting to say? You may think not. Don't worry; you're not alone in that. And there's no need to invent stories or become a different person; it's all about the technique in rewiring how you think about your own experiences in relations to those of others.

Many of us ASSUME that others are more interesting than us. We assume everyone else leads more interesting lives, right? We may have absolutely no evidence of this—we could even be meeting this person for the first time, and for all we know, he or she may be dreadfully boring.

One of the greatest daggers to our self-confidence and how we present ourselves to others is self-doubt. We'll dig into this more in later chapters. But the fact is, if you don't believe you have anything interesting to offer, then others will no longer find you to be interesting either. Trust me, you could say the most mundane thing, but if you have confidence in saying it, it's automatically more interesting. You can change the way someone else takes in information simply by using more expressive gestures, exuding confidence, and maintaining eye-contact as we've covered in previous chapters.

While we'll dive into improving your humor later in this book, let's consider stand-up comedians for a second, specifically observational comics. They can find humor in even the most ordinary aspects of day-to-day life. While their observations may not be particularly mind-blowing, it's how they deliver their material and find it *so* interesting themselves that naturally pulls in the audience, often drawing big laughs.

Jerry Seinfeld is famous for his observational humor. Consider this bit of his: *"We don't understand death. And the proof of this is that we give dead people a pillow."* This is a simple observation of an inherently non-funny subject and yet, we laugh. It's an interesting observation that we may or may not have made on our own, but Seinfeld's technique and delivery conveys a confidence in this joke that we're drawn to.

But I'm not a stand-up comedian! I'm no Jerry Seinfeld!, you may be thinking. That's okay! To be interesting doesn't mean you *have* to be funny; at least not all of the time. But if you want to always be interesting, then you should have some go-to stories in your arsenal.

Think about an interesting person at a party. Have you ever stood amongst a group of people who are all drawn to a particular person? Perhaps someone nudges them, and says, *Hey, tell that story! You know, the one where you missed a flight and had to hitchhike and ended up in the wrong country?*

While that sounds like the beginning of *quite* the tale, it certainly piques your curiosity. And consider the person suggesting this story: it's clear they've heard it at least once before—yet they found it so interesting that they believe it's worth hearing again for the sake of telling those who haven't heard it yet. People who know charismatic and charming people often want other people to know them too; people are excited to be able to say, "hey, this funny person is MY friend," right?

So, consider what makes YOU different or even what makes you similar to those around you. You may not think having worked in an ice cream shop is particularly interesting, but if you think back on your experience in doing so, there's probably a silly story in there.

Remember these words from Henry Ford: *"Whether you think you can or whether you think you can't, you're right."* If you're doubting yourself from the beginning, you're knocking yourself down before you've even had the chance to stand up. Much like dogs can sniff out fear, humans can absolutely sense self-doubt in someone else. It's easy to tell when someone is unsure, nervous, and lacks self-confidence. We see it in someone's eyes, appearance, actions, etc.

Okay, but what if you REALLY can't think of anything interesting that's happened in your life? If you don't already keep a journal (though you should, more on that later!), take a moment to write down an abbreviated timeline of your life. List out jobs you've had, places you've lived, any place you've traveled to—these don't have to be extravagant. You don't have to have gone to Paris or Greece to be an *interesting* person, despite what anyone else says or thinks. And you don't have to have worked in a big city or have had a near-death experience to be *interesting*. Remember that!

Of course, as you write down some highlights of your life, you still may think you have nothing interesting on paper. You've lived through all of these things; been there, done that, right? What's interesting about it now? Again, it's normal to feel that way. But you've been living your life, well, for your whole life! It's much like an author who has been working on the same book for years. They may re-read parts and find them boring or confusing...but they've looked at these words hundreds and hundreds of times over. All it takes is a fresh set of eyes to see that the book may in fact be <u>gold</u>.

Many stand-up comedians have this happen when they're writing and working on their sets. And so they "work out" material in smaller clubs and venues before they take on a bigger stage and massive crowds. On paper, they have jokes that they may be unsure of; they know that there could be *something* there but it's a question of what the crowd will ultimately think. When they "work out" the joke, they may find it got a bigger laugh than expected, or the opposite. It's all about perspective.

Of course, a joke may fail, and something that you thought was great and interesting may not come off that way to others. The same can happen with a story; this isn't just about jokes! If you've written down your accomplishments and still feel as though you're not interesting enough, don't worry.

Here are some keys to live a more interesting life so that you have more confidence, and you'll have greater power to engage with others as you move forward. Remember, you can't live your life waiting for others to take you with them on a grand adventure…you have to find a grand adventure of your own if you really want to. And, chances are if you're reading this book, then there's something in you—a fire, a <u>drive</u>—that's pushing you to become a funnier, more charismatic version of yourself.

Consider these questions that someone else might ask you:

What are you reading? Your answer: Well, I don't actually read much...

What do you do for fun? Your answer: Well, I sit at home and watch TV or play video games...

Yikes! While these may be fine hobbies, it may not be super *interesting* to others; of course, it all depends on your audience.

Now, you shouldn't do something that you genuinely don't *want* to do. No one wants to hang around someone fake or someone who is just putting on a front to try and *be* more interesting to others. People will spot you faking it from miles away. But if you find that your answers to these common questions are, well, lackluster...then people are going to find <u>you</u> to be lackluster. But if you find yourself always saying, *oh I wish I could do that* or *I wish I had time to try that*...then it's on YOU to make that time. Even if it's a half an hour a day to learn something new—always start with baby steps when creating goals for yourself. It does no good to overwhelm yourself. Plus, you don't have to be an *expert* in something to be more interesting to others. If you're confident enough to try something new and take yourself out of your comfort zone, people will appreciate and admire that.

Be open to try new things and expand your horizons; this way not only will *you* become more interesting, but you'll find that you come across more interesting people too. And sometimes the most interesting thing about someone is the other people they've met and the stories they can share vicariously through others.

An easy way to become more interesting is to get involved in something bigger than yourself. That can mean giving back and fighting for something you believe in is inherently interesting. If you volunteer for the local fire department or the humane society, that's something interesting too! People will want to know *why* you're drawn to doing work like that and what the connection is there. Perhaps they too know people who volunteer where you do. This also endears people to you because helping others shows that you're unselfish and kind. But, again, this has to come from a genuine place. If you're doing anything just for the gold star of doing it, folks will see right through you. And, honestly, that can be worse than doing nothing at all. It may be better to be a bore than to be a complete fake.

Of course, you can always take a class to learn something new; there are plenty of free online resources these days. Perhaps you're taking an online improv class, or you're taking French language lessons through the Duolingo app. You may already do these things and they may not pop into your mind when you try and think of something *interesting,* right? Many times, when people think of what may be "interesting," we automatically jump to these big, grand things, like cliff jumping, hitchhiking, traveling, performing, etc.

But even the smallest thing in your everyday routine can be extremely interesting to someone else. Do you have a plant collection? Do you love taking photos? Do you practice any instruments or enjoy redecorating? Perhaps baking is your thing. Or maybe you're really into handwritten letters and sending snail mail to friends, family, and strangers. Anything goes! There are only so many things one person can do, so chances are if you do *something* it'll be different than what someone else is doing—and *that* can be super interesting.

Plus, by even trying to do or learn something new, inevitably you'll have stories from that. Whether it is about your experiences or the people you meet along the way, just by *trying* something new, you'll already be ahead of the game in the "interesting" department. You'll have so many more stories to tell others! Just remember…don't overthink it. I know, easier said than done. And we'll talk more about the downfalls of overthinking in upcoming chapters.

You may not think you can *always* be interesting, but there's always going to be something interesting about you to anyone else. It's easy to get caught up in the day-to-day life and think everything is the same and mundane; but to someone else—someone YOU may see as interesting—they may see their life as rather dull and boring! Again, it's all about perspective.

Now, once you have some go-to stories, test them out on friends in social settings. Everyone should have at least three go-to stories that they can tell anyone at any time. They should be transferrable, meaning it shouldn't matter who the audience is. As an exercise, try writing down those three stories now. Start with an outline and think about what stood out to you—what makes the story interesting, funny, shocking, and/or unique?

If you want to take it a step further, try practicing telling the story in a mirror. Of course, you don't want to sound like you're reciting a script when you're talking to others, but you'll want to get used to the flow of the stories you wish to tell—especially if you tend to be more shy and less outspoken in a crowded room. All self-confidence starts from within. You need to be comfortable enough with yourself before you can shine in front of others.

Remember, you ARE interesting. You can captivate a room. You CAN be the most self-confident version of yourself and learn to make others laugh with ease. Now that you've got your stories, it's time to dazzle and *dash*!

Chapter 4: Dazzle and Dash

"If you can't dazzle them with brilliance, baffle them with bull." — W. C. Fields, American Comedian

The *dazzle and dash* is different than what you may know as the *dine and dash*, which is the act of skipping out on a dining bill...we definitely don't condone that! However, we know that *dashing* away can be a great thing given the circumstance. I mean, we all know that Prince Charming can be described as *dashing*, right? Well, maybe that's a different kind of dash...

The point is that the key to entertaining with confidence is to *always* leave your audience wanting more. And, as the great comic W.C. Fields says, if you can't dazzle with brilliance, baffle with bull. Whether you decide to dazzle those around you or end up baffling them, the point is to stand out and be memorable.

From going on a date to entertaining a crowded room, you want to leave folks curious about you, right? Again, it's much like stand-up comedy; comics love to end on a high note when the crowd is doubled over in laughter. *Dazzle and dash right off stage to keep people wanting more!*

It all goes back to having the ability to charm someone's socks off. You won't do so by being arrogant or pushy about something. You need to know when to exit with grace. Sure, you may have the attention of the whole room and you think, *I could go all night! These people are hooked by my every word.* But right when you begin to get cocky is when you could potentially lose the audience altogether. And once you lose a crowd, it can be very, very difficult to win them back.

TIP: A simple way to dazzle someone is to remember his or her name. It's extremely common for people to automatically forget someone's name immediately after they introduce themselves. Happens to the best of us! The key is to come up with a trick to remember names—as soon as someone introduces themselves, associate their name with something else.

Her name's Nicole? My middle name's Nicole! Perfect. Or my mom's sister's name is Nicole! As soon as you make this association, it'll be hard to forget. And while it may be a simple thing, remembering someone's name or a fact about them will go a long way.

Another key to the *dazzle and dash* is that it's imperative to know when to <u>share</u> the spotlight. If you want to win people over, you need to literally invite them into the spotlight with you and also know when to step away altogether.

Comedian Mike Betancourt reminds us of this simple truth: "When you leave on a high note people will always remember you. Unfortunately, when you leave on a bad note, they will remember that too."

If you're a *Seinfeld* fan, you may remember this scene from an episode called "The Burning." George is talking about *losing* a crowd and Jerry reminds him to leave on a high.

"**George:** I had 'em Jerry. They loved me.

Jerry: *And then?*

George: *I lost 'em. I can usually come up with one good comment during a meeting, but by the end it's buried under a pile of gaffes and bad puns.*

Jerry: *Showmanship, George. When you hit that high note, say goodnight and walk off."*

If you're a big fan of comedy and going to live shows, you may notice that many comedians will end their sets on a big laugh. Not only that, many comics will *dash* out of the venue following a good set—oftentimes, they're dashing off to another gig!

Of course, you don't want to dash away if all goes wrong. Maybe you stuck your foot in your mouth at a party or said something *funny* that didn't come off too well.

In that case, you'll want to address mishaps, failures, etc. Don't run away. People admire someone who can own up to a failed joke, or whatever it is, more than they admire someone who runs off to avoid facing people after the fact.

The main takeaway here is to know the difference of when to leave on a high note versus when to linger for a bit longer. If you're self-confident, and you're always making people laugh, people will continue to talk about you long after you leave a room.

Part II: Confidence Is Built From Within

"Sometimes, if you fake confidence long enough, you're going to be confident."
— Elle King, American Singer & Songwriter

In this section of the book, we'll talk more about building confidence. Where do confident people get it from? Why are some people so much surer of themselves, and why do others struggle so much with it?

As Elle King says, it *is* true that if you fake confidence long enough, it'll help you to build *real* confidence. Fake it till you make it! And in the words of beloved *Seinfeld* character, George Costanza, *"It's not a lie if you believe it!"* You've just got to love the fake confidence that George brings into his life.

Of course, the intention here isn't to go around spreading lies. You won't be a more interesting person by lying about your experience…well, you will be interesting for a bit, but the truth will always come out, and then your credibility will be shot. But if you believe yourself to be interesting even through the seemingly ordinary, then you'll become more interesting to others.

Confidence is all about how you carry yourself and what you believe about yourself and those around you. As you'll learn in the following chapters, self-confident people tend to share certain characteristics. And while some may come naturally, many of these can be learned.

Chapter 5: Sure I'm Sure? How to Be Positively Self-Assured

"*Because one believes in oneself, one doesn't try to convince others. Because one is content with oneself, one doesn't need others' approval. Because one accepts oneself, the whole world accepts him or her.*"
— Lao Tzu, Chinese Philosopher

We've talked about why charm is essential in the first part of this book. Now, let's take a deeper dive into building confidence and learning how to be more self-assured. If you believe in yourself, you're already ahead of the game. But, of course, many of us doubt ourselves again and again. We say "I'm sure" with a question mark rather than a period. Or we say *I think*…rather than *I know*.

So, do you think you're confident, or do you *know* you're confident?

It's easy to spot self-confident people; in fact, there are plenty of things to indicate a person is confident and self-assured. People who are self-confident do what they believe is right, even if mocked or criticized for it. They're more willing to take risks and go the "extra mile" to get what they really want. Plus, they're able to admit when they've made a mistake, and they're more than willing to learn from their mistakes. They know that it's better to admit to mistakes, because this will actually build up their credibility at the end of the day. Remember: real people make mistakes. Robots don't, but of course, robots are, well, *robotic*.

Self-confident people also wait for others to congratulate them on their accomplishments rather than bragging or boasting about them in an effort to shove something in someone's face. No one likes people fishing for compliments. Also, when compliments *are* given to these people who are more self-confident, they accept them with grace and gratitude. They don't automatically believe that they deserve all of the recognition; in fact, these people will often bring others in to share their spotlight rather than hogging it all for themselves. Again, they are confident enough to *share* their good fortunes with others; they don't feel the need to overcompensate.

Alan Mallory, an international speaker, author and performance coach, writes not only of what self-assurance means but also of how to live a more self-assured life.

"Self-assurance means knowing that we can and will succeed. Being able to say to ourselves (or others) during a difficult or stressful time, "It's OK. I've got this," is not only powerful but reassuring as well. It's important to assure ourselves that whatever is going on or is about to happen, it's going to be all right, because we have what it takes to get through it—at least at this moment in time. This opens the door to taking calculated risks in life. A self-assured person is willing and ready to take on a challenge or see the opportunity in something, knowing they can manage what comes their way. It's also fitting for those times when we volunteer to do a job at home or work, not because we're excited at the prospect, but because we know we can do it, in a good amount of time, and with

little difficulty. It needs to get done, and we're the person to do it. That's self-assurance.

Self-assurance is also a key aspect of resilience. We don't tend to give up when we're assured that we can make it in the end, and if we don't, that's ok too, because we know that new opportunities will be available and that we've learned from our experiences. We continue to pick ourselves up when life's situations knock us down because we have faith in our strengths, whatever they may be. We also don't feel diminished or threatened by asking for help; it's not a sign of weakness. We simply have things we aspire to; and asking for advice, guidance or a helping hand might be just what we need to get there."

Being self-assured also means we validate ourselves; we don't rely on others to endorse or support our feelings, thoughts, or experiences.

We're our own judge and jury! In today's world of social-media influences, this has never been more critical. We can have thousands of followers for example, and get more 'likes' than anyone else, but there's zero correlation between that and our self-confidence. For decades we blamed magazines and advertising for *"upholding dangerously unrealistic standards of success and beauty," but now it's far more prevalent because of social media. It's up to us to have and nurture our self-acceptance so that these external, superficial influences don't chip away at our self-assurance."*

Through all of this, Mallory reminds us that becoming more self-assured is a very achievable goal. And it's *definitely* worth the effort.

Not sure where to get started? Let's start simple! Check out the below tips to become a more confident version of yourself:

- *Try accomplishing small tasks as a start, and practice doing them well and on time—with no excuses! As your faith in yourself grows, so too will the challenge of the tasks. You'll take on bigger and better challenges over time, crushing them as you go!*

- *Make a point to observe the behaviors of other self-assured people. See if there's something specific they do—or don't do—that you can pay attention to. You can begin to mimic that behavior but don't strive to become a carbon copy of anyone else. Just apply what they do to your own life.*

- *Promote what's good about yourself as an individual, such as your character and values; not your looks, money, vacations, or possessions. Really focus on what's on the inside. It may sound cliché, but it's true…remember, you can't take anything with you on the way out of this life!*

- *Get into the habit of regularly practicing self-affirmations in an effort to continue to build yourself up. From writing positive sticky notes to stick on your mirrors to keeping a gratitude journal, there are plenty of ways to remind yourself that you are deserving and just an overall amazing, awesome human being!*

- *Be sure to take care of yourself. Remember, when we don't eat well, don't get enough rest, or drink too much for example, we know we aren't at our best, and we won't have the self-assurance to tackle those things that will make us feel better about ourselves. A strong body equals a strong mind...and a strong mind can do anything!*

As you begin to start putting the above points into practice, you'll find a newfound freedom in caring *less* about what others think and you'll start believing in yourself even more. And a funny thing will start to happen...people will actually be more drawn to YOU!

The less you care what others think, the more people will actually flock toward you. Remember, there's a difference between confidence and *cockiness*. If you're just living and enjoying your life, doing what you love to do, others will be *positively* drawn in. Again, don't overthink it! You do you and others will see that and love you for it!

Of course, it's important to remember that self-assurance can take time; simply reading these words won't magically make you a more confident person. It will take diligence and practice like anything else. It also means surrounding yourself with others who will work to bring you up rather than down.

Take a moment to look at those around you—how do they treat you? How do they treat *themselves*? This can be rather indicative of how you view yourself, especially in a group presence. If you're self-conscious in front of the people whom you call your friends, then that says something, right? Do they bring out the best in you? Do they encourage you? Or do they doubt you because they're just following the lead you've given them in doubting yourself? OR do they doubt you because they don't think they could do it themselves, and therefore transfer that self-doubt to you?

These are all important questions to ask yourself! Don't surround yourself with people who will perpetuate your feelings of self-doubt. Seek out those who will lift you up and encourage you to pursue your dreams and tell your own story. Simply being around people like this will help you to build your own self-confidence.

Next, we'll talk about breaking down your walls in order to build up your confidence. It's easier said than done, but it's definitely possible, just like anything else! Onward!

Chapter 6: Breaking Down Walls to Build Up Our Confidence

"Walls protect and walls limit. It is in the nature of walls that they should fall. That walls should fall is the consequence of blowing your own trumpet."
— Jeanette Winterson, English Writer

One of the biggest keys to becoming more confident in yourself and drawing others in is to truly be in touch with who you are, both inside and out! It's impossible to let others in if you don't work on yourself first. And the fact is that most people enjoy being around vulnerable, open people.

The more you release, the more it allows others to share their biggest hopes and fears with you as well. If you're open about your own journey, you will automatically create a safe space for others to join in and discuss theirs as well.

One of the greatest hindrances to building self-confidence is the "story vs fact" mindset. Once you understand this concept, you'll be able to get over so many mental hurdles, and you'll be drawing in people in no time!

Story VS Facts

It's so incredibly easy for people to get swept up in their own internal narratives, right? *What will they think of me? They must think I'm crazy. I can't do that or else...or what if...*

We've all been guilty of overthinking and creating these crazy, endless *stories* in our heads that may prevent us from doing things *in real life*! For example, you might create a story in your head that you aren't funny and that no one thinks you're funny. Maybe you texted someone a joke and they never replied, not even an "lol," and now your mind is spinning—they didn't think you were funny, ah! However, you don't know the *facts*. Perhaps, that person meant to respond but became distracted. It could really be as simple as that. Try not to spiral!

If you find yourself confused, just remember this quote by Eckhart Tolle:

"Every ego confuses opinions and viewpoints with facts. Only through awareness—not through thinking can you differentiate between fact and opinion. Only through awareness are you able to see: There is the situation and here is the anger I feel about it, and then realize there are other ways of approaching the situation, other ways of seeing it and dealing with it."

When we consider this, we can soon realize that what we hear, repeat, or believe, may not always come from true, factual information. Many inspirational and motivational speakers remind us of this: don't believe everything you think!

That may sound a bit kooky at first, I know. But really consider it. Many types of thoughts prevent you from living your best life. For example...

- Fearful thoughts may narrow your thinking and ultimately prevent you from taking action.

- Stressful thoughts can create discomfort and take you away from living in the present moment. Whether you're stressed about the past or future, most of the time you can't control whatever it is that you're stressing about!

- Anxious thoughts can create unpleasant feelings about the future. While anxiety can pop up for many of us, it's essential be able to recognize these thoughts and know that they usually don't serve our best interests.

- Distracting thoughts can pull your attention away from the things that really matter to you.

REMEMBER: Most of the time, your thoughts are just STORIES that you tell yourself to try and make sense of this crazy world we live in. All of the stories we have our based on our own experiences and interpretations, however, they're not always based in REALITY.

You may be spinning out in your head over something that's completely, well, made up in your head! Untrue "stories" can mislead us; oftentimes, these stories can even perpetuate limited beliefs, create judgments, and prevent us from taking action.

As Business Development Coach Jamie McKenna said, *"Stories we believe, which are not based in fact or assumptions we make about others, can contribute to feelings of low self-worth and keep people in a state of disempowerment and negativity."* This is why both our inner and outer dialogues are SO important for not only how others perceive us, but how we perceive ourselves! This impacts our emotional well-being, as well as our mental and physical health.

If you keep telling yourself a story that you're not going to amount to anything, you're not funny, you're not charming—well, guess what? That *story* will soon gain legs and become true, because you'll never have the confidence to prove yourself wrong.

However, if you keep telling yourself the opposite: you're funny, likeable, people are drawn to you, etc., then your chances of building self-confidence are that much higher. Whether you like it or not, sometimes you've just got to *fake it till you make it!* It's a tried-and-true technique, trust me!

Need a little help on where to start in terms of breaking down those walls to build confidence? Below are five tips from recognized psychologist expert, Dr. Janice Webb.

1. **Open up:** As children, many of us are brought up to "be quiet" and not interrupt others—especially adults. The key here is to override the unspoken childhood rule that tells us, DON'T TALK. Identify those in your life whom you find to be trustworthy and talk to them about difficult things in your life and difficult things in their lives. Open up about things you never would have before. Be vulnerable. Talk, talk, and talk some more. The more you open up, the more others will open up, and this will build confidence both ways. Plus, you may find that you're able to laugh at situations that perhaps you once found embarrassing or shameful. You'll be surprised to find out how many others have

gone through whatever it is you've experienced!

2. **Don't deny your emotions:** Make it a habit to, several times each day, close your eyes, focus inward, and ask yourself, "What am I feeling?" Pay attention to how you feel about things, and really *listen* to those feelings. Know that your feelings matter. If the feelings that come up are difficult to handle, you can always find a trained therapist to support and help you learn to tolerate and manage them. By making friends with your emotions, you'll be more in touch with who you are and how you come off to others. Plus, you'll have a better understanding of what others may be going through, making you more relatable and approachable overall.

3. **Take your own needs seriously:** Many of us tell ourselves stories that we're unworthy of help or that we're overreacting when it comes to certain situations. The key here is to override the unspoken childhood rule that

says, DON'T ASK. Learn to tell the people in your life when you need help or support, and then let them help you. Letting others help you will ultimately help you to serve others in the future. Life is all about give and take; it's truly cyclical.

4. **Let people in:** You'll never be the most confident or funny person in the room if you're ice cold. You need to let people in. Fill your life with quality people. Meaningful relationships are a primary source of richness, connection, and overall meaning in life. Plus, you'll learn to draw on these connections to tell better, more interesting stories; leading a lone, solitary life can only get you so far.

5. **Get to know who you are:** Pay attention to everything about yourself. What do you love, dislike, excel at, struggle with? What is important to you? What are your values? What do you care about? Once you see the full picture of who you are, you will see your value and worth, and you will feel stronger.

Once you start to get over the initial hurdles of opening up, you'll find a new world of possibilities waiting for you! Don't overthink it...actually, if you have trouble with the whole overthinking thing, you'll be happy to find the next chapter addresses that exact topic.

The walls and hurdles built up in your mind are only as strong and tall as you allow them to be. We have the power to control all of our actions, even if we can't always control our thoughts. But there are plenty of techniques we can put into play. Let's learn more about the key to quell overthinking!

Chapter 7: The Key to Quell Overthinking

"When you've had a life of overthinking, you have the same reaction time and time again. Shyness becomes habitual. When you're put in an unfamiliar situation, all you want to do is retreat and hide by default. You watch but don't participate. You listen but don't respond. You read, but rarely comment. You take a photo, but you rarely post. You write, but you rarely publish. All of this is because your overthinking mind cannot stop thinking about how you will be perceived by the outside world."
— Joel Annesley, Life Coach & Author

Tying into the previous chapter, now we'll dive deeper into the poison that is *overthinking*. Of course, overthinking is an extremely common phenomenon; so many of us are overcome with manifestations that solely live in our own minds…so, how do we get over that? Well, it can be tricky.

Let's consider comedy again. The thing is most professional comedians are also "professional overthinkers." Comics see the world in different ways; they muse on things that "normal" folks might simply not notice at all. So, in that sense, overthinking can be a positive; in fact, it can lead to a whole lucrative career!

However, overthinking can also prevent us from accomplishing certain dreams and desires. The key is to recognize when you're going down a *negative* spiral of overthinking, and then learning how to quell that. Do you constantly second-guess yourself in a crowded room? Are you always playing the comparison game? It's time to get out of your own head!

Take it from Tony Robbins, American author, coach, speaker, and philanthropist. Tony says, *"Whatever you hold in your mind on a consistent basis is exactly what you will experience in your life."* This is something that the world's most successful people realize—and the only difference between them and everyone else is that they have learned how to harness the power of their own *thoughts* to help them achieve.

According to Robbins, the classic overthinking definition is, *"to think about something too much or for too long."* While it's human nature to think things through when making a decision or evaluating a situation, it quickly becomes **overthinking** when you can't get out of your own head.

Of course, this happens to *all* of us at some point in our lives—we all experience events that cause us to become very worried or stressed out. Plus, the older we get, the more we see how things can go *wrong* and that life is far from perfect.

That's normal. But some people can't seem to turn their concerns off. They worry about the future, and they constantly think about potential catastrophic events—no matter how unlikely they may be. It's easy to get swept up in a world of "what if's," but that's no way to live. Remember, none of us make it out of this crazy thing called life alive anyway!

Overthinkers may also ruminate about the past, often beating themselves up about "should haves" and "could haves." They may fret over what others might think about them and/or they may let negative self-talk build up in their minds. That's a sure way to destroy your self-confidence.

Sometimes overthinking a tough decision you have to make can also cause problems. Replaying all the options in your head can lead to what's known as "paralysis by analysis." You may be SO afraid to take the wrong action that you end up taking no action at all. But you must remember that even making the wrong decision is better than making no decision at all! It's absolutely natural to make mistakes—that's how all of us learn. Remember, even the most self-confident, funny, successful folks had missteps too. There's no straight and narrow path to success.

Think back to when you were a kid…did you think about *anything* before you took action? Probably not so much, *right*? You just went into anything and everything, guns a blazing. You had no fears because you didn't have much life experience to draw from—there really was nothing *to fear* at that point.

Naturally, as we grow older, we realize that we can play it safe or take some risks. We look to others for advice and those who may serve as examples. While the risky decision may not always be best, it'll definitely teach us something either way. But if you overthink a decision for too long, you may risk not taking any action altogether...and that's no fun when you're on your death bed, right? Everyone wants a life filled with experiences and bold decisions; a life worth talking about.

Problems associated with overthinking can lead to way more than just inaction. Whether you're a chronic overthinker or you're in a spot where you need to make a tough decision, you've probably experienced sleepless nights when your brain just won't turn off. Overthinking can also increase symptoms of depression, elevate your stress levels, and cloud your overall judgment. Yikes! Not good!

Okay, so we've talked a lot about the detriments of overthinking, and you may feel a little overwhelmed. While there still may be moments where you find yourself thinking *too* much on something, there are tips to help you quell overthinking. Let's dig deeper into that.

The first step to quell overthinking is to learn to take control of your own story.

This goes back to the last chapter when we discussed the difference between stories and facts. While stories are often rooted in fiction, it's imperative to take control of yours and know what's true and what's not…no matter what others may think or say about you. You have to trust yourself and what you know to be true. Don't let others' doubt lead you to doubt yourself!

Tony Robbins says, *"We are all telling ourselves stories. The question is, does your story empower you or does it hold you back?"*

Now, let's tie this into overthinking. Overthinkers may tell themselves, "well, I've always been a worrier" or "I'm just naturally more anxious than everyone else." These are *stories* that hold you back and can be especially hard to change if you've never asked yourself, "wait, WHY do I overthink?"

Perhaps you were raised by parents who didn't play sports, so they didn't think to get you involved in sports either. So, you grew up to naturally believe you weren't athletic, because you never participated in sports. However, that's a story you've created for yourself. Now, as an adult, you may be reluctant to try a sport…even if you REALLY want too deep down. But you've created this false narrative. Ah, what's a person to do!?

To overcome your limiting beliefs, you need to first IDENTIFY them. Then, you can catch yourself when you start telling yourself these negative stories! By doing this, you can work to replace them with positive ones, like "I am in charge of my body, my mind, and my emotions." Once you change your story (which you absolutely have the power to do!), you'll soon change your life.

The next step is to **LET GO of the past**. It's common for most overthinkers to focus on the past, expending energy on all of the "what ifs" and "should haves." Those who understand how to stop overthinking know that the past is just that. It's the PAST, it's gone! Done! And it can't be changed.

The only thing you can change is the meaning and value that you give to your past experiences. Everything is a learning opportunity. Letting go of the past means that you don't let your mistakes control your future decisions and you don't dwell on everything you did or didn't do. It's so important not to let bad things or experiences control your current emotions. For example, you can always forgive others and let go of your anger. This is truly one of the most significant ways you can change your story.

    Piggybacking off of that, you may not be surprised that the next piece of advice to quell overthinking is to **LIVE in the moment**. We've all heard it before, right? Just try to live in the moment; focus on the here and now! While it may sound cliche, it is true that living in the moment is KEY to learning how to stop the overthinking machine in your mind.

Of course, most people can't just flip a switch and live in the moment...but what if they could? The truth is that you can take control of your mind and stop negative emotions in their tracks. Again, think about the most self-confident people you know; the people who can really light up a room. Do you think they spend much time dwelling on the past or do you think they enjoy living in the moment? If you're stuck in the corner at a party focusing on something you said three years ago, you're missing out on everything and everyone who is right in front of you.

It's critical to be able to identify overthinking before it spirals out of control. Take a moment to reset your mind; breathe and focus on the present moment. Take a look at what's around you. Ground yourself by using all of your senses: What are you seeing? Smelling? What do you have to be grateful for right now? There's probably more than you think once you start listing them out!

Keeping daily rituals, like meditation, can really help you to prime your mind into being more aware of the present and focusing less on the past which can lead to the overthinking spiral. You CAN retrain your brain to live in the moment, just like most kiddos do. Soon you'll find it comes naturally as it did in days before.

Make no mistake that living in the moment doesn't necessarily mean that you should bury any negative emotions you may have. Of course, your past is a part of who you are; it's how you've gotten to where you are today. Both the ups and the downs shape us into our present selves. And every bit of the journey is important.

But to really master all of your emotions, you need to take time to acknowledge them; really identify their root causes. If you're unsure of how to do this, or it's too overwhelming, you may want to consider talking to a therapist. Therapy is a great way to evaluate certain emotions and other feelings and thoughts you may be having. If you find yourself feeling sad or anxious, dig into that. You'll find that by digging deep rather than ignoring it, you'll be able to release these negative energies rather than keeping them bottled up.

Tony Robbins reminds us that *"it's often about facing your larger fears, such as not feeling in control of your life or not progressing in a way you'd like to be. Become aware of the root causes of your overthinking and you can start making progress to stop it before it starts."*

And as Tony says, *"Identify your problems, but give your power and energy to solutions."* You've identified the real reasons for your stress and anxiety, but your work isn't done. The only way to learn how to stop overthinking once and for all is to take charge of your life. If your overthinking is caused by stress at work, you may want to rethink or reconsider your career path. Does your job bring you joy? Do you worry what others will think if you leave your job for something you really want to do?

If you're not where you want to be in life, take time to set goals for yourself so that you can get there. If you feel like your life is totally out of your control, you must make the decision today to get back behind the wheel. It's not always easy. These are BIG moves, and they take guts. But remember that no one else has control over your life and what you can make a reality.

Don't worry about what society says or what this person will think or what that person will say. If you want an extraordinary life, if you want to be more confident, if you want to make others laugh and bring joy to the world, you CAN do that, and you WILL do that.

If you find yourself overthinking everything a lot, you may find that you also have difficulty distinguishing between the *fear* of making a mistake and the potential mistake itself. Think back on a time when you were afraid to do something—were you afraid of the actual thing or what the potential outcome would be? Let's go back to stand-up comedy: say you've never done it before, but you really want to. However, the fear of failing is crippling—what if the audience doesn't laugh? What if they heckle? Worse, what if they're totally silent? Sure, these are all *possibilities*. But you can't overthink outcomes that haven't even happened! The most you can do is mentally prepare yourself and then go for it...you'll deal with whatever the outcome is when it eventually presents itself. Nobody—NOBODY!—can predict the future.

"Knowing if fear or intuition is guiding your behavior will help you get out of your head and take the next necessary steps," said Tony Robbins. *"By connecting to your body, taking a few deep breaths and really feeling what it would be like to make a decision, you can decipher whether fear or intuition are in play and how to best move forward."*

Do you ever ask yourself WHY you are overthinking? Like, why am I just constantly overthinking this or that situation? Why can't I just live my life and go with the flow? Why am I so stuck on this? While it's good to recognize the fact that you ARE overthinking, it's not super helpful to ask WHY or to dwell on that. Chances are, you'll just continue to overthink on the issue of overthinking—yikes! It really is a vicious cycle.

Rather than questioning all of your overthinking, take time to focus on more proactive and solution-oriented questions.

For example, instead of asking yourself "Why do all of my relationships become unpleasant over time?" ask instead "What energy am I putting out there that keeps attracting negative partners?"

Asking questions that allow you to make changes to your own behaviors will help you to move forward in a healthier manner. You'll soon find that you can ultimately reduce overthinking and improve your life. You may still have moments where you overthink…but don't overthink it!

Now that we've learned to quell our overthinking brains, it's time to have a bit more fun. If you want to build your confidence, you must tap into your more poised and playful side!

The next chapter will dig more into that so you can learn when and how to know how to carry yourself in any given situation so that, no matter where you are, people will still be drawn to you. It's all about the energy you give off!

Chapter 8: Poised and Playful

"I feel like I play with good poise and I know when to take my shot—and when I do, I have a lot of confidence." — Joe Harris, American Basketball Player

Concluding Part II of this book, let's talk more about confidence! We've considered all of the negative things our minds can do; dwell in self-doubt and spiral into bouts of overthinking. But now it's all about being both poised and playful, and when to know the difference in what's needed given any situation you find yourself in.

Think about your favorite celebrities or just people you may know personally; if they are charming and self-confident, chances are they also know when and where to be *poised* as well as when and where to be *playful*.

This also ties into knowing *how to read the room*, which we'll discuss in upcoming chapters. But the key to being poised and playful is to not be strictly one or the other—no one likes somebody who is serious ALL of the time, just as nobody likes someone who must be the class clown or jester ALL of the time. Both can get old rather quickly.

Again, consider those that you view as sophisticated and self-confident. They have a certain air to them; a pleasant aura. They're mindful of others as well as how they present themselves.

To be self-confident doesn't mean you need to be the loudest, most obnoxious person in the room. Oftentimes, it's just the opposite of that. You can be silly and fun while being generally more quiet and less in-your-face than others.

To be poised and playful is to be approachable. When you're in a room filled with people, do you silo yourself off? Or do you create a space for people to come up to you? It's all a balance and for some it's more natural a dance than others. But awareness is always the first step in learning anything!

Watch what others do; take cues on when to insert yourself and when to back away. We'll keep this chapter short and sweet, just as you should be when you're working on self-confidence and making people laugh.

Part III: Joke's on You: I'm Funny!

"**Henry Hill**: You're a pistol, you're really funny. You're really funny.

Tommy DeVito: What do you mean I'm funny?

Henry Hill: It's funny, you know. It's a good story, it's funny, you're a funny guy. [laughs]

Tommy DeVito: What do you mean, you mean the way I talk? What?

Henry Hill: It's just, you know. You're just funny, it's...funny, you know the way you tell the story and everything." — Goodfellas

Now that we've built up your confidence and given you the keys to succeed both inside and out, we'll really start to dig into finding your funny bone!

In this section, we'll discuss how to find humor in nearly *every* situation…find funny everywhere! We'll also dive into the delivery of jokes—timing is everything. And finally, how does humor convey confidence? We'll take a look at why certain funny people appear more confident and why we're drawn to these people…and, of course, how you can become one of the funny folks who draws people in!

Again, don't let others create the narrative for you. Even if someone says, "you're not funny"… don't take that as truth! Even if you're not meant to be a stand-up comedian, everyone can draw on wit and charm to add a funny bit or comment to a conversation. Sure, it comes more naturally to some than others—but now's not the time to doubt yourself.

You've already come this far! Read on to learn more about finding humor in every *little* thing!

Chapter 9: Finding Humor in Every Little Thing

"Humor is perhaps a sense of intellectual perspective: an awareness that some things are really important, others not; and that the two kinds are most oddly jumbled in everyday affairs."
— Christopher Morley, American Journalist

Let's consider humor and *funny things* in the first place. The key to being able to make people laugh easily is to know *how* to find humor in simple, everyday situations. Knowing how to draw that humor into social situations will have folks flocking to you continuously.

First of all, many people think that they're not funny because nothing funny happens to them. You may hear a stand-up comedian tell a hilarious story and think, man, that could ONLY happen to them! Nothing like *that* ever happens in my boring, ordinary life…well, that's where you're wrong!

There is humor everywhere, in all of our everyday lives. You just need to be open to finding it—and then sharing it with others.

If you want to inject more humor into your life and the stories you share with others, you'll want to start by creating a habit of humor. *What the heck do I mean by that?* Well, it's a way to actively look at the funnier side of things in your day-to-day life.

Set a goal for yourself to write down <u>three</u> funny things you observed each and every day. Maybe it's something that happened to you personally, or it was a funny story you read in the news. It could be an observation or a personal anecdote. Anything goes!

You know what really helps here? Don't OVERTHINK it! Aha! We talked about that already, so you should know how to quell those thoughts by now.

Draw on what we talked about in earlier chapters…if you thought it was funny, write it down! If it made YOU laugh, make a note of it! Don't overthink on whether or not someone else will think it's funny, etc. Sure, sometimes we do have "you had to be there" moments, but there are plenty of other funny events that we can share with others in social situations.

Remember, *not everything has to have a punchline*. Humor can be found in the simplest of life's observations. Here are some ways to incorporate finding humor into your life.

"Humor is everywhere in that there's irony in just about anything a human does." — Bill Nye, "The Science Guy"

Take Note of What Others Miss

Have you ever heard a cliche or familiar phrase but realized you have no idea what the origin story is behind it? For example, "it's the bee's knees" or "it was blown to smithereens" or "paint the town red." You may know the implied meanings of such phrases, but do you know their actual meanings and origins? The average person may wonder, but they don't care enough to dig deeper.

Be the person who digs deeper. Find the humor in these familiar phrases! Or, make up your own origin stories. What does "paint the town red" mean to you? How could you put a hilarious spin on that? Play around with these ideas!

Curate Life's Contradictions

There are SO many things that truly make no sense when you just dig a bit deeper. For example, George Carlin has a great joke about dogs. *"Dogs hate it when you blow in their face. But put them in the car and they stick their heads out the window."* It's a simple observation that makes everyone laugh because it's so ridiculously true! Make note of these things and start pointing out these contradictions to others; see what others find funny and keep them in your "story arsenal" to bring up with others.

Challenge People's Assumptions

Assumptions constitute the foundation of joke structure as the mechanism of misdirection. Without an assumption there can be no misdirect; and without misdirection there can be no surprise.

Start to tune in to what others have assumptions about, then surprise them with an unexpected alternative. Jokes often come from shattering assumptions. Just when you think someone's going one way, they spin around and hit you in the funny bone when you least expect it!

Don't Dismiss the Details

Remember when we discussed how many comics are overthinkers? Comedians notice things that many others simply pass over; and not only do they *notice* things, they really dig into them. The beauty of comedy is in the details, so pay attention to them. Seemingly irrelevant pieces of information you experience everyday can be fodder for jokes. Comedians note those insignificant details that others can't be bothered with.

Investigate Things You Dislike

Comedians talk about things they think are wrong. So, make a point to really study the enemy. Things that annoy you can serve as premises for your greatest jokes. Some comedians make a whole living off of "rant-style" comedy; it's often relatable and others laugh because it's true.

Professional comics will also willingly put themselves into situations that are less than ideal, purely for material. For example, accepting jury duty, helping someone move, letting your mother-in-law live with you for a bit, etc.

Know the Latest Trends

To find humor in everything, you need to be familiar with what's relevant. Again, people find things funniest when they are *relatable*. Your jokes really need to hit home for others to find them funny. This means you may have to try out trends that you otherwise wouldn't. Perhaps that means online dating, sporting a new fashion trend, etc. If it's something out of your comfort zone, even better—it's sure to make for a silly story!

Look Back on Historic Events

Looking for content to play around with? Well, luckily, the history books are chock full of interesting stories and events in which you can put your own unique, comedic spin on! Famous comedians often use historical events in their material as metaphors. This is also a way to really stand out, because most "creatives" don't typically study history in traditional education programs. So, by doing a bit of research, you can really stand out from the rest of the pack.

Be a Playful Contrarian

Have you ever agreed with something but disagreed for the sake of a fun argument? Oftentimes, great storytellers and comedians will do this too, just to get a rise and reaction from the audience. However, this technique can quickly become irritating, depending on how often you use it—you don't ALWAYS want to be the person who HAS to go against the grain. But pissing people off can really teach you how much others care about their opinions and beliefs. For example, even if you're a theist, be an atheist in conversation for a day. Dislike chocolate. Again, even if you deep down don't agree with what you're saying, being able to explore the other side will open your mind and allow you to dig deep on all sides, furthering your connection with others. Remember, the typical *average Joe* avoids confrontation and will just be a "yes man" which can be pretty boring.

What's Going on in Pop Culture

Even if you're not "into" pop culture, it's certainly a way to stay relatable and have some material to draw on if need be. For example, are you familiar with all the products for depression, ED, bad breath, dry skin, sore feet, etc.? Have you noticed any themed stories on the news? Take topics that others may have seen but then find a way to spin them into something different and/or funny.

Research is KEY

Comedian Mark Normand loves to say, *"give it a Goog"* when referencing looking something up on Google. If you don't know something, Google it! Have you ever thought about what people used before toilet paper? Give it a Goog! Corn cobs? Seashells? Yikes! Talk about nature's pooper scooper! Funny observations can lead to interesting rabbit holes if you know how to do the proper research. Open a book every once in a while, too! You'll find that you suddenly have so much interesting information to draw on.

Sit, See, and Serve

One of the greatest things you can do to become more self-aware, self-confident, and funny is to simply sit back, listen, and OBSERVE. Then, *serve* those observations to others in a humorous way. Become more aware of the world around you.

Go to your favorite park, coffee shop, or bookstore. Use all of your senses to observe what's going on around you. Listen for funny pops of conversation or even others' observations. You'll quickly notice so many things you've taken for granted or ignored over the years. The world is an amazingly diverse place filled with infinite possibilities. There are realms the average person never notices.

You totally have the ability to find humor in all of life's craziest situations, and even the most mundane. Life is silly—we shouldn't take it so seriously. Humor helps us to heal, and it is the great unifier. Laughter is the same in every language!

If you're the person who can find humor in even the most ordinary situations, you'll be the person who people want to be around more and more.

Someone who can look around and find even the most mundane things humorous is a person who can find joy in the little things in life. This is someone who clearly enjoys the moment, rather than waiting for it to end. And this person can spread that joy to others.

YOU can be that person. All you have to do is tap into it and nail the delivery.

Chapter 10: It's All in the Delivery

"The world is a tragedy to those who feel, but a comedy to those who think."
— Horace Walpole, English Writer

When it comes to being funny, it's all about the delivery. Knowing how to "read a room" is essential if you want to make others laugh. Of course, the "room" may be just one other person with whom you're engaged in a conversation with.

No matter the size of your crowd, it's imperative to know *how* to deliver whatever it is you're trying to say.

Remember, while your material is certainly important, how you <u>present</u> that material is also important. Sometimes, your delivery can outshine the material itself. In fact, think of the lamest joke you know. Now, if you put a different spin on it in terms of how you tell it, you might actually find that it can get laughs.

With a good delivery you get laughs, but a bad delivery? You could get heckled, or worse—you could be swimming, or drowning, rather, in dead silence.

Of course, the above refers to performing actual stand-up comedy; however, the same is true if you're just telling a story in a normal, social situation, say, at a party. Think about a person you've seen who has absolutely captivated those around them; now, consider what he or she was actually talking about. Was their story REALLY that funny? Or was it just the way the person DELIVERED the story? Were they gesturing a lot? Using a silly voice or accent to convey the tale? Sometimes, it's not so much WHAT the person is saying, but quite simply *how* they are getting the message across. A very charismatic person can make any story great just by having a stellar delivery.

In an ideal setting, you want to have both a compelling story AND a super-duper delivery. Sometimes, to nail a delivery it's all about pausing before certain parts—in fact, this is known in the industry as a "comedic pause."

Comedian Milton Berle has actually made fun of delivery and timing in his own jokes on stage. One audience member said, "He'd do a setup and a punch, the laugh would go up, and as it peaked, he would say, 'two, three, four' and start the next joke. He was making fun of the timing of it."

Do you want to be better skilled at delivering and timing your stories in a social setting? Do you want folks to be drawn in and truly captivated by what you have to say?

Consider these tips on delivering great material and stories from blogger and self-proclaimed funny man, Andy of *The Naked Speaker*.

The first thing you say to anyone is important; remember, first impressions are everything! The first three sentences out of your mouth should be punchlines if you really want to wow a crowd. Of course, if you're just in a more casual social setting, the aim is to get a laugh out of someone from the start.

It could be a quick-witted observation or one of your three main stories you have in the arsenal. Once you get someone to laugh, you'll have them on your side.

Try to hide your nerves. I know, I know. Easier said than done, right? But if you want others to see you as a confident person, you certainly can't be shaking in your boots. Internally, you might be…but best not to let others see that. Nerves can manifest in a variety of ways—from a shaky voice to a sweaty palm. The only way to get over these things is with practice. Keep putting yourself out there! Smile and breathe—I promise you'll get through it!

Be mindful of people's time. A surefire way to lose a crowd is to drone on and on about something…especially if it's not even interesting to begin with! This is where it also helps to know how to read a room…you can usually tell when someone is losing interest in a story. If you want control of a room, you don't have to monopolize the time. Remember to be poised and playful. Share your stories, make people laugh, but also let others into the spotlight…and allow people to step away from a conversation gracefully. No one wants to be held hostage in a conversation!

When telling stories, the most important thing is to be true to yourself. You can be a quiet, shy person and still come across as confident and funny. The moment you try and be something you're not—say, loud and super expressive with your hands—then people will know you're just trying too hard to get their attention. Again, there is always a line when it comes to confidence and staying true to who YOU are. The point of this book is not to recreate a person that you can't identify as yourself; it's just about learning to recognize certain thoughts and feelings, and how to convey them in a way that's true to you.

If you feel like you're trying too hard or playing too much into a role that you think others want or need, take a step back and reevaluate your delivery.

Be mindful of your audience, maintain eye contact when talking to people, and remember that what you're saying has value—don't let anybody make you feel otherwise. You're allowed to take up space and time and to fill a room with joy and laughter.

And why is that important? Humor is one of the best ways to convey confidence…and this book is all about building self-confidence and making others laugh. So, let's dig deeper into these ideas.

Chapter 11: How Humor Conveys Confidence

"Whenever I eat at a restaurant I never put the napkin in my lap. People say, 'Hannibal, why don't you put the napkin in your lap?' Because I believe in myself. I believe in my ability to not spill food in my pants 'cause I'm a goddamn adult. And I've mastered the art of getting food from my plate to my mouth without messing up my jeans. You need to believe in yourself, too and get your life together, that's for babies. Have some confidence in your eating abilities and hand/eye coordination."

— Hannibal Buress, American Comedian

Alright, we've learned more about this whole *funny business* thing...but how and why does humor convey confidence? Why is it that funny people appear to be more confident than others?

The Wharton School of Business recently found that people perceive those who have a facility for humor as more confident and competent than those who don't feel as comfortable telling jokes.

See?! It's just science!!

Additionally, it's been reported that laughter in humans evolved to signal safety. According to researchers, hominids millions of years ago laughed during fleeting periods of safety to promote social interaction which ultimately led to strengthening group cohesion. This instinctive laughter later on developed into conscious, controllable laughter and this is what we use today to signal friendliness! Who knew that laughter served an evolutionary purpose?

Humor is a great tool to make important points. Think about your favorite class or lecture or even TED talk that you've watched...chances are, the speaker used humor at one point or another to grab your attention and keep you focused on the topic.

Funnily enough, the most confident people are often those who have mastered the art of self-deprecating humor. Being able to poke fun at yourself is a sign that you're actually quite confident in yourself...confident enough to draw attention to your flaws and make fun of them. The simple truth is that nobody is perfect...so why pretend to be? Better to acknowledge the negatives with humor and laugh along with everyone else!

Humor is also a great way to forge real, genuine connections with people as a way to balance both confidence and credibility. Think about various bosses or leadership teams you've had to deal with over the years. Some bosses can come across as being wildly intimidating; they may often shut people down and make others feel bad. Now, think of a boss who was friendlier...what made this person friendly? Chances are, he or she peppered humor into their day-to-day to lighten the overall mood.

Humor works to cut through tension, and it relaxes people, opening them up to listening. While it isn't appropriate to use humor in every situation, there are certainly ways to find opportunities where you can inject humor to help balance both your credibility and influence. People love funny people!

It also takes a certain amount of courage to be funny; you're putting yourself out there in a way that's more vulnerable, right? You could easily sit back and let others take the spotlight, trying to joke around with others. You could play the silent observer for the rest of your life. But where's the fun in that?

Humor also conveys confidence because it allows you to be more genuine. And genuineness can open people's minds and hearts to your overall message.

Sometimes the funniest folks are just the people who are simply being themselves. They may not even consider that they're "funny"... they're just keeping it real and living their lives.

When you're feeling down or "not good enough," remember that humor conveys confidence like nothing else. If you feel some tension in a room, try cracking a joke! It may or may not land, but at least you had the confidence to try. People will always appreciate that.

Remember: A leader who uses humor conveys confidence. A leader who uses humor conveys a sense of trust. A leader who uses humor creates likability. You can be that leader!

Of course, you may have to fall off the ladder a few times before making it to the top. We'll talk about how falling down is the key to success in the next part of this book.

Part IV: Falling Down Is the Key to Stand-Up

"It doesn't matter if you fall down; everyone does. What matters is what you do next. You either stay down or rise up again. That's what determines your strength."
— Nadine Sadaka Boulos, Ph.D. Educational Technology

One of the greatest keys to comedy is knowing that you'll need to take a few falls in order to stand back up again. As with anything else in life, learning something new is always a bit of trial and error.

Of course, the more you keep at it, as long as you're determined and strong-willed, you'll be on the road to success.

In this section, we'll discuss how to stay humble, how to tap into those endless stories to keep people engaged, and how bruised egos can actually help to *build* confidence!

Chapter 12: The Humble Comic

"You have to have a big vision and take very small steps to get there. You have to be humble as you execute but visionary and gigantic in terms of your aspiration. In the Internet industry, it's not about grand innovation, it's about a lot of little innovations: every day, every week, every month, making something a little bit better." — Jason Calacanis, American Entrepreneur

When it comes to comedy, it's so important to stay humble. And that goes for just overall likability and confidence as well. No one wants to be around a show-off or somebody who thinks they are the greatest gift on this planet.

No matter how funny you are and how big of a crowd you can gather, always stay humble! This is especially true of professional comedians; it's crucial to remember that, without an audience, you wouldn't be able to even practice comedy.

Be mindful of who you are addressing and those around you, whether or not you're practicing comedy. If you're always just looking to have the spotlight on you, but you have nothing worthwhile or interesting to say or contribute, people will see right through you.

Don't focus so much on what you're saying or whether or not it's actually funny; try and relate to those around you and just focus on making them feel good—because that's what it's all about!

Again, it's about living in the moment. Don't think too much about how you look or what others may think.

You can build confidence by building up others around you; once you start to come off as if you're better than others, that's when you'll lose everyone.

Remember, humor that serves only to draw attention to YOU is what's known in many a grade school circle as "showing off." And as we remember from those days, nobody likes a *show-off*. In fact, show-offs can shove off as far as we're concerned! It's always a good idea to indulge in a little self-analysis.

Chapter 13: You've Got Endless Stories

"We are, as a species, addicted to story. Even when the body goes to sleep, the mind stays up all night, telling itself stories." — Jonathan Gottschall, American Scholar

Many people think they have nothing funny to say and they freeze up—but we all have endless stories to draw from. In this chapter, we'll dive more into how to tap into those stories.

As we've talked about in previous chapters, no matter how uninteresting you think your life is, there's somebody who will find what you have to say interesting. Remember, we all come from different walks of life and what you may deem to be "boring" may be super fascinating to another.

Many of us get caught up in overthinking, but if you read the chapter about that, you'll know that it's critical to recognize and stop that cycle from taking over. You DO have stories to tell, and you CAN tap into them in any social situation.

You've lived a whole life and you have way more living to do—every second, moment, day, week, and year is a new adventure. It's your story! I promise you hold more than you could ever know.

Don't believe me? Start *listening* to others more. What are they talking about? What kinds of events are they drawing on when they are telling stories?

Watch some stand-up comedy specials on Netflix...what are the most popular comedians drawing on? Usually, the topics are quite familiar and relatable. Simple tales of life at home or growing up in a certain part of the country can have audiences doubling over in laughter.

Why? Because these are the stories that bring us together; whether they're relatable (so we see ourselves in them), or so wildly crazy that we can't even imagine ever being in such a situation. Either way, we're laughing.

Whether you're an only child, a middle child, a parent of three, a cat mom, an iguana dad, etc., you have your own unique life story to draw from in any social situation. People often get so caught up in their minds thinking that they have nothing interesting to contribute, when that's just not the case at all.

Sharing our own experiences is what makes us human—it's how we've evolved as a species. We learn by sharing stories with others, right? Don't worry so much about comparing yourself to what Joe or John or Jodie has already done in his or her life...you've got your own unique life to live!

If you're really stuck on how to share a story of yours with someone else, just think of it like a movie script. Consider the art of telling a story as creating a movie inside the mind of your audience—even if it's just one other person. What should you describe or talk about so that they can really see what you're saying? Hook them into your story and then run with it! You've lived it after all! The more you share with others, the easier it will become over time.

Okay, so you know that you HAVE stories, but how do you convey them to others? That can be the trickiest part, right? Here are some tips to charm folks and appear more confident in your storytelling abilities:

1. Inject emotion into your stories.
2. Create a fun rapport with the audience.
3. Use a good story structure; try not to jump all over the place or else you'll risk losing people's attention.
4. Keep it personal and bring the characters and scenery to life!

Think about the best stories you've heard from the most confident people you know. They can take the most mundane story ("I went to the grocery store and bought eggs and went home.") into the most captivating tale you've ever heard.

Inject color and life into your stories—and remember to keep an open mind and eyes wide open as you go about your day-to-day because THAT'S where your stories come from, right? If you're just letting life pass you by, then of course you're not going to have anything interesting to say. You have to be open to receiving all of the quirky little joys that life has to offer you. And then you can share those pleasures with others.

Of course ... it's not always fun and games.

Chapter 14: Bruised Egos Build Confidence

"As humans, we often let our egos rule our decisions. We let fear stop us from reaching our true potential. We forget about love. But the heart, it never forgets. No matter what happens, no matter how hard things get, it always remembers." — Liz Fenton, Author

Of course, not even Jerry Seinfeld or Larry David can be funny all the time, and you certainly can't win everyone over all the time. But that can actually make you FUNNIER. In this chapter, we'll talk about the confidence boost that can actually come from a bruised ego.

Every (successful) stand-up comedian must take many a fall before seeing his or her name in lights. Similarly, this can go for anything in life. If you want to build up your confidence, you must take risks. And that may mean making mistakes along the way— mistakes that can make you look silly, ridiculous, even stupid, or ignorant. It happens to the best of us!

Of course, it's all about learning to take these falls in stride, picking yourself back up, and carrying on. If you take a seat and keep crying over the past and reopening old wounds, you'll never be able to heal and move forward.

Take Ari Shaffir for instance. He is an extremely successful and very funny comedian, actor, and host of the podcast *Skeptic Tank*. And his approach to failure is simple: *"Failure isn't a lack of success. Failure is just a process that leads to success."*

Ari goes on to say *"To me, every time it [performing stand-up] goes badly I see it as a good thing because that means I'm one step closer to where I want to be."*

It's true that the best stand-up comedians are like mad scientists, honing their craft bit by literal bit. Remember that failure is just a step in the grand scheme of succeeding. The most confident people in the room have failed...and, most likely, they will fail again. But their ability to remain poised, calm, joyful, and mindful about it all is what keeps them focused and at ease around others.

Also, remember that failure can be subjective. If you're a comedian, a joke may have "failed" because it was the wrong crowd, or the audience was distracted by something else happening in the room. Failure isn't always a straight line; there are often other factors. And sometimes you can *think* you failed, but others will think the total opposite!

Comedian Emily Winter reminds us that "strength doesn't come from burying feelings and ignoring losses; it comes from embracing them. As comedians, we need to feel the pangs of rejection, because they're important: They signal us to grow and change. Every failure is life instructing us to make an adjustment."

So, go on and be unabashedly unafraid to risk bruising that ego of yours. We're all on this journey together, and the sooner you realize that, the sooner you'll be able to relate to others and draw them in rather than cause people to distance themselves from you.

Next, you'll finally learn how to *make people laugh*. Is it easier said than done...or is it just plain easy?

Part V: Make People Laugh

"I have not seen anyone dying of laughter, but I know millions who are dying because they are not laughing." — Dr. Madan Kataria, Medical Doctor

For the final part of this book, we'll revisit the main point in the title: make people laugh. That's why you're reading this book, right? You want to know how to *make people laugh!*

In this section, we'll talk about the fact that you can't fake funny. Additionally, we'll dig into the importance of humor in relationship-building (it's more crucial than you may think!), as well as how to choose your comedy style and run with it.

There are SO many types of humor—from family-friendly to dark and self-deprecating. We'll figure out which is best for you and how you can draw on this humor in any situation.

Chapter 15: You Can't Fake Funny

"I prefer to surround myself with people who reveal their imperfection, rather than people who fake their perfection." — Charles F. Glassman, Author

While my motto is "fake it till you make it," you can't actually fake funny. In this chapter, we will talk about how you don't have to lie to be funny and you certainly don't have to make up scenarios. Not everyone can be a stand-up comic, but we can all tap into humor to build confidence.

No one likes someone who is fake; the key to comedy is finding an authentic humor. What makes YOU funny? You may have no idea! But the fact is you must go through trial and error, testing jokes and stories on others, to see what hits home for people. But you can't try TOO hard or make everything up—people will see right through that.

People love funny people. That's just the plain old facts. And whether they're truth-tellers or joke makers, the truly funny individuals in our lives deliver much-needed, crucial relief as important as any prescribed medicine we could get.

But how do you avoid being *that* person...you know who I'm talking about. The one guy or gal who makes others *cringe* at the very prospect of them cracking a joke? The one who laughs loudest at their own (perceived) comedic brilliance?

We all know that type, and most of us can feel our innards clench as soon as they open their mouths because we know how uncomfortable and awful their jokes are going to be.

And then, there are those who can walk into any room, give it a quick scan, and make an observation SO funny, one would think it HAD to have been planned. You want to become one of THOSE people. *But how?*

Well, it's a lot of what we've already talked about! Don't try too hard. Read the room. Invite others into your conversations and stories. Practice warmth and graciousness—don't be rude or think you're better than anyone else. Empathize with those around you, and ASK others about themselves. Always be listening and search for the unique humor in everyday events or observations. If your eyes and ears are open to every potential silly thing around you, you won't need to be fake at all. Natural humor will come easy to you if you just allow it in.

And just like you can't fake funny, the best comedians will tell you to never fake a laugh. If you don't think something's funny, we don't want to hear your fake laughter!

Take it from Australian comedian, Joe Avati:

"Ever had to fake a laugh? I'm one of Australia's top comedians...I can tell when someone's faking it. It's something we all have to do at one point or another in our lives, whether in response to an offensive joke told by a prominent client or an awful pun during dinner at

your in-laws. If you think you were getting away with it, think again. It turns out that people can tell when we fake laughter—and there's even research to prove it.

Research was undertaken at the USA's UCLA into the art of faking laughter, and it found that two-thirds of all fake laughs are detectable by listeners. Fake laughter can even be detected by those as young as five years of age! When we fake a laugh, we breathe differently and use different vocal muscles than when we actually, instinctively, laugh. This difference in sound is something most humans can detect subconsciously, even if we can't put our finger on what exactly is off.

As a whole, we seem to be moving beyond faked laughter in all its forms. And it's about time, I say! Not only are we better at detecting a fake laugh, but we are also less inclined to be told what is and isn't funny. Just take a look (and listen) at most sitcoms on television today—unlike the shows of the eighties and nineties—the canned laugh track dubbed over often really funny comedians is rarely used to guide the audience responses, leaving them to decide for themselves if the jokes are humorous or not.

Not only are you fooling nobody when you fake a laugh, but you're also forgoing the real benefits of laughter when you fake it, such as boosting your immune system, decreasing stress and releasing endorphins. When we find a good comedian genuinely funny (even if it's not me), our brains respond with pleasure, but when we hear a fake laugh, our brains instead try to decipher what the fake laughter means.

In the end, faking a laugh does nobody involved any favors. You aren't having a good time (and neither is anybody else), and nobody wins. You're better off discussing which comedian you both find funny and enjoying one of their live shows together rather than trying to force someone to attend a live comedy show of a comedian that only you find funny. Here, neither of you will feel pressure to laugh at something that isn't funny, and you can relax and have fun."

We can get through life faking a lot of things, but laughter certainly isn't one of them. Fake laughing isn't even fun! The greatest thing about laughter is when it comes from the gut and has you doubled over, barely able to breathe!

Don't try to be someone you're not. You can take advice from others. You can inject their practices into your own life. But you always just have to be your authentic self. Laughter will come easily if you're just REALLY real. That's what it comes down to.

Chapter 16: The Importance of Humor in Relationship Building

"Shared laughter signals that they see the world in the same way... Perceived similarity ends up being an important part of the story of relationships." — Sara Algoe, Researcher

Why is it that SO many people say that the number one thing they seek in a romantic partner is a sense of humor? Why is humor SO important in building relationships? Well, the ability to be silly and funny is a big deal!

Being humorous not only can build trust and confidence, but it's nice to be around people who don't take everything SO seriously all of the time! Life has crazy ups and downs and if we can't laugh about it along the way, what's the point?

Humor is one of the greatest tools we have for improving one-on-one relationships. Consistent use of humor makes other people want to listen to you. Think about it this way...who would you rather go to lunch with? The guy in accounting who only talks about how stressed he is about work and his family, etc. or the girl in sales who always has an entertaining story to share? The choice seems pretty simple!

Think about your favorite person in any environment you've been in. Who was your favorite teacher? Your favorite boss? Co-worker? Person you've dated? What do these people all have in common? You may find that each one of them was funny, or at least had a stellar sense of humor.

Think back on how you made friends in school...many of the greatest friendships are forged over shared laughter. It's like a secret code. Oh, you think this is funny, too? Great! There's probably something here worth exploring.

Victor Borge once wrote *"Laughter is the closest distance between two people."* Many of us would probably agree that laughter brings us closer to others, whether we're joking with our spouse or laughing with an audience at a comedy club.

Researchers at the University of North Carolina at Chapel Hill actually devised a way to produce shared laughter in the lab, to measure experimentally how it might impact a relationship with a stranger.

The study goes further to say:

"Participants watched a funny, not-so-funny, or not-funny-at-all video while supposedly video-chatting with another same-sex participant. Unbeknownst to them, the video chat displayed a pre-recorded clip of someone laughing the same amount for each of the two funny videos, but only smiling occasionally during the unfunny video. This produced more shared laughter in the first scenario, minimal shared laughter in the second, and no shared laughter in the third (but still a positive interaction).

Afterward, the participants then filled out questionnaires about their positive and negative emotions, their sense of similarity to their video partner, and how much they liked or wanted to get to know their video partner.

Results showed that, across the different videos, the amount of shared laughter had consistent effects on the participants' sense of similarity to the video partner—and that this, in turn, increased how much participants liked their partner and wanted to affiliate with him or her.

For people who are laughing together, shared laughter signals that they see the world in the same way, and it momentarily boosts their sense of connection," says social psychologist Sara Algoe, co-author of the study with Laura Kurtz. *"Perceived similarity ends up being an important part of the story of relationships."*

"These results align with two other surveys they conducted, where participants recalled and answered questions about a recent interaction they had—this time, with someone close to them. When they reported more shared laughter (compared to unshared laughter), participants said they experienced more positive emotion and less negative emotion during the interaction, saw the person as more similar to them, and were more satisfied with the relationship. This held true even when controlling for other factors that might

explain the good feelings, such as the length of the relationship and number of verbal and physical expressions of love."

Remember, this goes back to caveman times! Laughter was a way to signal safety. Laughter is the common thread in every corner of the world. There's a reason people hang those super-cliche signs in their homes: live, laugh, love. That's all we really want in life!

Think about how contagious a smile is. Well, you can't laugh without smiling—don't even try it!

Next, we'll talk about choosing your uniquely confident comedic style…and then you'll be off to the races! Get out there and use everything you've learned in this book.

Chapter 17: Choose Your Style and Run with it

"Comedy is a reflection. We create nothing. We set no styles, no standards. We're reflections. It's a distorted mirror in the fun house. We watch society. As society behaves, then we have the ability to make fun of it." — Alan King, American Actor

If you've read this book up to this point, thank you and congratulations on making it to the final chapter! Hopefully, you've learned some useful tools that you can begin to implement in order to become more self-confident and to make people laugh in any situation.

Whether or not you're looking to become a professional comedian with this book, it's imperative to know what comedic style you have. Do you tend to be drawn to dark humor? Are your jokes more family-friendly? Is your style more self-deprecating? Is your humor more about the delivery or the content? Do you have good comedic timing, or do you rely solely on your charisma and charm to get by?

No matter your style, the key is to just be authentically yourself. While some comics find joy in poking fun at themselves for the sake of getting a laugh, others may not enjoy that style as much.

While you DO want to *read the room* and understand your audience, that doesn't mean you need to change the core of your comedic style and who you are to make someone else laugh or feel comfortable.

Remember, there ARE lines. You need to know that not everyone will find you funny, and even if you do become the most *charming person in the room*, there will be an outlier or two who don't agree. And that's perfectly okay! The goal of this book isn't to learn how to win everyone over.

First and foremost, your style should make you comfortable. If you don't like to curse, then you don't need to curse to be funny. What works for one person won't necessarily work for you. And remember: people can spot a fake from across the room! Don't play into what you THINK people want to hear from you and don't just try and copy what others are doing.

Some people take on a bit of a comedic persona when they're on stage, or even when they're entertaining a small group of people. Whether it's a lilt in their voice or a more dramatic way of gesturing, having a persona can be a lot of fun to draw others in. However, like anything else, it's not for everyone.

If a comedy persona comes naturally to you, great. But just know that it can take years to develop a comedic persona—it's rather challenging and you shouldn't necessarily strive for it if you're just looking to be more self-confident and make others laugh. However, if you're looking to perform professionally then you may want to try improv and other ways to dig into other potential personas.

According to Comedy Gold, *"your persona is what makes your jokes your jokes. Anyone can write a joke about parents or dogs vs. cats or homework or taxes or gentrification or doughnuts. But only you can write a joke about your unique take on those topics."*

Think about your favorite comedians. Do you associate a certain persona with them? Is his or her humor more dry? Dirty? Silly? Do they use props?

There are six main styles of humor to keep in mind when choosing a style of your own, or really *discovering* what your natural sense of humor is. These include observational, satire, deadpan, dark, surreal, and slapstick humor. Let's dig into each one a bit more, with examples of comedians for each.

Observational Comedy: Observational comedy is a form of humor based on the commonplace aspects of everyday life. It is one of the main types of humor used in stand-up comedy. In an observational comedy act the comedian will make an observation about "something from the backwaters of life, an everyday phenomenon that is rarely noticed or discussed." Famous comedians known for their observational wit include the likes of Amy Schumer, Joan Rivers, Kevin

Hart, John Mulaney, Ali Wong, Phoebe Robinson, and Jerry Seinfeld.

Satire: Satire typically relies on what's *trending*. From important news and headlines to current affairs, satirists poke fun and dramatize these events. This type of comedy dates quickly, but is extremely popular for use in late night talk-variety shows. Seth Meyers, Jimmy Kimmel, and Jimmy Fallon often use satire in their sets.

Deadpan: While deadpan isn't strictly a *style* of comedy, it's a funny way of telling jokes. For instance, take Aubrey Plaza and Christopher Walken. They're so skilled at saying something hilarious without changing their facial expression or outward emotions at all. If you can say something truly funny without cracking a smile, that can often be the funniest thing of all!

Dark: Dark humor certainly isn't for everyone. Sometimes people draw on their own life situations to deal with trauma in a humorous way. This humor often deals with disturbing subjects such as death, drugs, terrorism, rape, war, horror, etc. However, if you can make these topics funny, it can really win over a crowd. The idea of getting an audience to laugh following a cringe or gasp is a really unique experience. Not every comic can pull it off.

Surreal: This is a form of humor that's based on bizarre juxtapositions, absurd situations, and nonsensical logic. If you're someone who often makes up worlds in your own head and if you love tall tales and stories of fiction, you may find that surreal humor is a great way to inject some funny into your day-to-day conversations. People may call you "weird" but, hey, the best folks are a little nutty!

Slapstick: This includes physical comedy like tripping, falling, practical jokes, mistakes, or highlighted over dialogue, plot and character development. If you love Seinfeld, you'll be familiar with Kramer's use of physical comedy in the show.

Of course, your style of "funny" doesn't have to fit into any one of these boxes. You can be a person who is just, well, funny and pleasant to be around. You don't have to be *known* for being dark or deadpan.

The end goal is to know what you're comfortable with, what makes sense for you, and what will draw others in when you're working to build up your confidence.

You are uniquely YOU and you have the power to captivate anyone! Trust that and run with it.

Conclusion

Are you laughing yet? Are you making others laugh? Laughter IS the best medicine, and it doesn't have to be a crazy journey to get a prescription for some funny in your life.

Remember, the point of this book comes back to its title:

How to Make People Laugh

And, hopefully, you've learned that it doesn't have to be that hard! The key is to tap into everything that you are and the world around you! There is so much to observe and share with others.

You don't have to put people down to build yourself up. You just have to break down your own walls and let others in. Be vulnerable. Be open. Be yourself. Be mindful.

Confidence doesn't equate to arrogance. And it certainly doesn't mean you always need to be the loudest person in the room. In fact, you can be a funny, confident wallflower! Don't let society dictate your inner thoughts, and don't feed the stories in your mind that cause spirals of overthinking.

Remember: don't believe everything you think! Our thoughts aren't always in line with reality.

If you need to *fake it till you make it*, then that's okay too. Start by telling yourself that you are self-confident and that you can be funny, and you can win over any person or crowd. Soon enough, that will become a reality.

Don't fall into the pits of self-doubt or comparison culture. That will do nothing to serve your self-confidence, and certainly it will make it way harder to make others laugh if you can't even find joy or laughter in yourself.

Thank you for reading this book and, if you've learned anything, be sure to share it with others!

Resources

Thank you to all of the researchers, motivational speakers, doctors, comedians, and others who've written about building self-confidence online and in print. This book has drawn on many great minds and below you'll find some of the resources used in writing this book.

www.bustle.com/articles/191027-11-interesting-habits-of-charming-people-according-to-experts

www.danieltrichards.com/being-charming-4-principles-to-make-yourself-more-alluring-and-persuasive/

www.quora.com/What-makes-people-charming

positivepsychology.com/self-confidence-self-belief/

www.alux.com/live-interesting-life/

alanmallory.com/2018/09/self-confidence-self-assurance/

goodmenproject.com/featured-content/what-being-a-comedian-taught-me-about-humility-and-loss-dg/

greatergood.berkeley.edu/article/item/how_laughter_brings_us_together

www.humorthatworks.com/benefits/building-teams-and-relationships/

https://goldcomedy.com/resources/5-ways-discover-comedy-persona/

https://coachcampus.com/coach-portfolios/power-tools/jamie-mckenna-facts-vs-stories/

http://nakedspeaker.com/2012/04/06/ten-tips-for-better-comic-delivery/

https://rz.mdrt.org/html/2017ampro-strategic-humor-for-leaders/

https://www.inc.com/jeff-haden/it-took-this-hilarious-stand-up-comic-just-1-sentence-to-give-best-advice-on-failure-ever.html

www.ingramcontent.com/pod-product-compliance
Lightning Source LLC
Chambersburg PA
CBHW071456070526
44578CB00001B/360